So You're
Having a
Mid-life Crisis!

Mike Haskins & Clive Whichelow

summersdale

SO YOU'RE HAVING A MID-LIFE CRISIS!

Copyright © Mike Haskins and Clive Whichelow 2009

Illustrations by Ian Baker

The right of Mike Haskins and Clive Whichelow to be identified as the authors of this work has been asserted in accordance with sections 77 and 78 of the Copyright, Designs and Patents Act 1988.

Summersdale Publishers Ltd
46 West Street
Chichester
West Sussex
PO19 1RP
UK

www.summersdale.com

Printed and bound by Tien Wah Press, Singapore

ISBN: 978-1-84024-734-3

TO..

FROM...

INTRODUCTION

You're not as young as you used to be, you're not as fit as you want to be and you've got a great future behind you. Don't worry; it's only a mid-life crisis! There, does that reassure you? No, thought not.

The fact is it's all in the mind, at least what's left of it. You've read somewhere that as you get older your brain cells are dropping off the perch at a rate of about 10,000 per day. Plus, your body is going to seed; too much TV, not enough TLC, all jam and no gym. Yes, we know, been there, done that and got the XXXL T-shirt.

And now you're starting to compensate. Better late than never, you think, and you're right. You can tone up that body, do a bit of brain training, buy some nice clothes, 'hang out' at some trendy joints and start feeling good about yourself again.

But... (there's always a 'but' isn't there?) Beware! If you start dressing like a teenager you probably will be hanging out – literally. All those bits you've been covering up for years will be popping out like curious campers peeking from a misshapen tent.

And is it really necessary to go out and buy a 500 cc motorbike or a pink sports car and roar around the town like a haggard Hell's Angel or a latter-day Lady Penelope?

You want to keep the years at bay, but with a bit of dignity, decorum and lashings of fun along the way. Reading this book may save you from embarrassment, humiliation and foolishness, but mainly it will save you from yourself.

Don't continue your mid-life crisis without it!

TELLTALE SIGNS YOU'RE HAVING A MID-LIFE CRISIS

You studiously avoid socialising with anyone over 40

You start looking for sexier, more exciting replacements for the following: your car, your partner, your hormones...

All your clothes are now made of
leather... including your pyjamas

You look like you're auditioning for a
lead role in a production of *Grease* that's
being staged in a retirement home

You start wearing skimpy swimwear,
even though you no longer have a
skimpy body to go with it

A MID-LIFE CRISIS IS...

... wanting to be less of a role model
and more of a supermodel.

... living it up without being
able to live it down.

... wanting to have it large but not wanting to get any larger.

... believing you're still more hip hop than hip op.

MYTHS ABOUT
MID-LIFE CRISES

They are based on irrational fears
– what's irrational about looking in
the mirror and being horrified to
see one of your parents?

No one else knows you are going through one – who else would buy trousers so tight that they can barely get them on?

You will never be able to re-capture your youth – you might if you hunt him/her down in your brand new, super-fast sports car

Your attempts to look younger will make
you look ridiculous – the natural process
of getting older probably will too –
just in a different way

It's a natural part of getting older
– what's natural about dyed hair, tummy
tucks, and facelifts?

CONVERSING WITH OTHERS (WHAT THEY SAY AND WHAT YOU HEAR)

'You're looking really good.' = 'My God! It must have cost you thousands.'

'So you're getting out and enjoying yourself a lot these days?' = 'You're going to give yourself a heart attack.'

'You seem to have plenty of energy.' = 'You're on some form of medication, aren't you?'

'Miserable weather we're having.' =
'It must be playing merry hell
with your arthritis.'

'So how old is your boy/girlfriend?' =
'I wish to establish that they are young
enough to be your son/daughter before
telling everyone you know.'

CONVERSING WITH OTHERS (WHAT YOU SAY AND WHAT THEY HEAR)

'Hello' = 'Hello, I am a young person – honest!'

'This phone line's a bit faint.' = 'I'm as deaf as a post.'

'Would you like a dance?' = 'I need someone to help hold me up'

To a 20-year-old of the opposite sex: 'Hi, what do you say to going out on a date?' = 'Any objections to me spending my entire life savings on you over the next two months?'

'I'll just have the soup, please.' = 'I
can't chew anything at my age.'

THINGS THAT COULD PROVOKE A MID-LIFE CRISIS

After running for a bus, you find you need a couple of days to recover

You get more enjoyment out of a box of chocolates than you do from the person who gave them to you

You try to recall all those wild sex and drugs orgies you had in your youth and realise you forgot to have any

You see a photo of Jack Nicholson/ Madonna with a younger partner and think, 'If whippersnappers like them can get away with it, so can I!'

YOUR NATURAL ENEMIES
WILL NOW BE...

People who just assume that
you're a grandparent

Anyone who fails to tell you how great
you're looking... for your age

People who are older than you but
manage to look at least
five years younger

Friends who are counting down the
years until you receive your bus pass

Anyone who reminds you of your age

CHAT-UP LINES YOU CAN USE AS A MID-LIFER

'Would you like to see my pension projection?'

'They say the finest wines are in the oldest bottles – fancy a vintage tipple?'

'Don't tell me you'd turn down an opportunity to help the aged?'

'Go out with me and I'll be able to help you with your history homework on the 1960s.'

WEEKLY HIGHLIGHTS DURING YOUR MID-LIFE CRISIS

Successfully squeezing yourself into
those jeans you used to wear
20 years ago

Starting yet another new wonder diet

Chatting up that nice assistant in the chemist when you go to pick up your prescription of hormone replacement drugs or Viagra

YOUR NEW OUTLOOK
ON LIFE

Maturity is overrated – let's
have some fun!

Stand out from the crowd – just because
everyone else your age is old, doesn't
mean you have to be as well

Having the body of a 20-year-old is
not impossible – it just may
not be your own!

You only live once – but who says you
can't be a teenager twice?

HAIRSTYLES AND ACCESSORIES FOR THE MID-LIFER (FOR HIM)

Ponytail – the implication presumably having something to do with stallions?

A Ferrari key fob – regardless of what car you actually drive

Plenty of bling – more than P. Diddy and
Sir Jimmy Savile combined

Odd, spiky haircut – that looks as though a hedgehog has been run over on your head

The completely bald look – which you hope others will assume you've adopted out of choice

HAIRSTYLES AND ACCESSORIES FOR THE MID-LIFER (FOR HER)

'Sexy' black tights – to hide those varicose veins

A loosely worn belt – so it fools people into thinking you have a girlish figure

The bright purple, red and blue spiky
hairdo – or, as it's better known,
the menopausal parrot

Bleached blonde hair – so bright that people can still find you in the nightclub during a power cut

A thick mane of glossy, youthful and healthy hair – and not only that, it's machine washable too!

YOUR LIFE WILL NOW CONSIST OF...

... lying about your age, unless it gets you cheaper car insurance.

... increasing body maintenance with diminishing returns.

... trying to get rid of, undo, recycle or get a refund on every bit of rubbish you have accumulated in your life over the past 25 years, starting with your partner.

... acting as a full-time, unpaid, human guinea pig for every anti-ageing product on the market.

... telling everyone about the *real* you (because no matter how long they've known you, none of them seem to have encountered this youthful character before).

THE CAR OF THE MALE MID-LIFER

One that reaches 60 even faster
than you're doing

Plenty of horsepower – just
like you, you old stallion

Satnav – despite your best efforts this may be the only sexy female voice regularly heard in your car

Bucket seats – always handy if you get caught short on a long journey

Open-topped – it lets you feel the wind blowing through your hairpiece

THE CAR OF THE
FEMALE MID-LIFER

Special in-car shoe wardrobe – that is
why they call it the boot, isn't it?

Bright pink bodywork – yes, even your
car blushes to be seen out with you

One that breaks down with surprising regularity so some young, hunky mechanic can come to your rescue

Secret compartment – to hide your driving glasses the moment you stop

Satnav – with a deep, sexy male voice that you can imagine is giving you directions back to his place

IDEAL GIFTS FOR
THE MID-LIFER

A distorting mirror that makes you look
permanently thinner

The services of your own personal
body double to save you over exerting
yourself at moments of excitement

Clothes with smaller size
labels stitched in

A Dorian Gray-like portrait of
yourself to keep in the attic

A speak-your-weight machine that lies

TRUTHS YOU WON'T APPRECIATE HEARING

All this effort to recapture your youth has made you look at least 20 years older.

Your youthful boy/girlfriend is actually just as old as you are but has been to a much better cosmetic surgeon.

Not only do you look like mutton dressed as lamb, it's a lamb that has no taste in clothing.

THINGS THE MID-LIFER
FEARS MOST

Old photographs of you coming to light
that prove you were alive some decades
prior to what you've previously claimed

Mirrors in brightly lit changing rooms

Being seen with any contemporaries
who have made no attempt whatsoever
to hide their state of advanced decay

WAYS YOU MIGHT REINVENT YOURSELF

As a sex guru now ready and willing to share your lifetime's erotic experience with the younger generation

As an 85-year-old who has worn exceptionally well

As an artists' model, so people will have to look at your flabby body whether they like it or not

As a colourful character, although not just because you have developed high blood pressure

As a living legend… or, failing that, just living!

NEW HOBBIES YOU CAN CONSIDER

Etching – so you can invite unsuspecting young people back to see your work

Leatherwork – that's what you'll call getting dressed in the morning

Travelling – you'll have no choice;
everyone within a 50-mile radius will
know far too much about you

Rambling – and perhaps dribbling too

Needlework – or DIY plastic surgery as it's otherwise known

Pottery – a potter in the garden followed by a potter round the shops

MUSIC YOU MIGHT HAVE STARTED LISTENING TO

Sultry, sexy soul music to try and get some of those under-used parts working

Rap music with offensive lyrics that your parents wouldn't like (unless you're Kelly Osbourne)

High energy dance music to try and get your heart rate back to what it was 20 years ago

WAYS YOU NOW DESCRIBE YOUR AGE

The wrong side of 30

In the prime of life

Experienced

Twenty-one again

WAYS YOU NOW MEASURE OUT THE REST OF YOUR LIFE

By the length of time it takes your successive partners to get too old for you to be interested in them any more

In hip replacements

By the length of time between
your Botox injections

THINGS YOU WON'T ADMIT TO

The terrifying amount you are shelling out to maintain your lifestyle

It's only because of Viagra your body remains vertical at all

That you look a bit daft in clothing
meant for someone 20 years younger

Having grown-up children,
let alone grandchildren

That your supermarket trolley is a very welcome means of support

OTHER NAMES FOR A MID-LIFE CRISIS

A sudden late surge of hormones... Yeah, right! From the chemist!

Adultlescence

The second age... or is it
the fifth or sixth?

Getting back in touch with
your inner teenager

HOW TO DENY YOU'RE HAVING A MID-LIFE CRISIS

'I have to wear leather trousers because I'm allergic to all other fabrics.'

'No, it's not a mid-life crisis. I've been so busy I've only recently managed to fit in becoming an adolescent.'

'My friend was having a mid-life crisis so I'm faking one to make them feel better about it.'

LOOKING ON THE BRIGHT SIDE OF YOUR MID-LIFE CRISIS

It sure beats an old age crisis!

At last! You now have something to blame all your daftest behaviour on.

It's Mother Nature's way of saying
'Enjoy yourself!'

www.summersdale.com